Serena and Venus Williams

by A. R. Schaefer

Reading Consultant:
Dr. Robert Miller
Professor of Special Education
Minnesota State University, Mankato

CAPSTONE
HIGH-INTEREST
BOOKS

an imprint of Capstone Press
Mankato, Minnesota

Capstone High-Interest Books are published by Capstone Press
151 Good Counsel Drive, P.O. Box 669, Mankato, Minnesota 56002
http://www.capstone-press.com

Library of Congress Cataloging-in-Publication Data
Schaefer, A. R.
    Serena and Venus Williams/by A. R. Schaefer.
    p. cm.—(Sports heroes)
    Includes bibliographical references (p. 45) and index.
    Summary: Traces the lives and tennis careers of sisters Serena and
Venus Williams.
    ISBN 0-7368-1054-4
    1. Williams, Serena, 1981– —Juvenile literature. 2. Williams, Venus, 1980– —
Juvenile literature. 3. Tennis players—United States—Biography—Juvenile literature.
4. African American women tennis players—Biography—Juvenile literature.
[1. Williams, Serena, 1981– 2. Williams, Venus, 1980– 3. Tennis players.
4. Afro-Americans—Biography. 5. Women—Biography.] I. Title. II. Sports heroes
(Mankato, Minn.)
GV994.A1 S58 2002
796.342'092'273—dc21   2001003634

Editorial Credits
Matt Doeden, editor; Timothy Halldin, cover and interior designer; Katy Kudela,
    photo researcher

Photo Credits
ALLSPORT PHOTOGRAPHY/Al Bello, 4, 16, 24; Sean Garnsworthy, 7;
    Gary M. Prior, 9, 40, 42; Ken Levine, 10, 13, 15; Clive Brunskill, 21, 26;
    Stu Forster, 34, 39; Adam Pretty, 37
AP/Wide World Photos/Elise Amendola, cover
SportsChrome-USA/Rob Tringali Jr., 19; Bongarts Photography, 23, 28, 31; Empics, 33

1 2 3 4 5 6 07 06 05 04 03 02

Table of Contents

Chapter 1 Victory in Paris 5

Chapter 2 The Early Years 11

Chapter 3 Professional Tennis 17

Chapter 4 Grand Slams 27

Chapter 5 Serena and Venus Today 35

Features

WTA Records 9

Career Highlights 43

Words to Know 44

To Learn More 45

Useful Addresses 46

Internet Sites 47

Index 48

Victory in Paris

On June 6, 1999, Serena and Venus Williams were playing in the women's doubles final at the French Open. Martina Hingis and Anna Kournikova were their opponents. Serena and Venus were seeded ninth in the tournament. Hingis and Kournikova were seeded second. Few people expected the Williams sisters to win.

Serena and Venus played their best. They won the first set 6-3. They then took a 4-1 lead in the second set. They were two games away from the title. But rain then started to fall on the court. Officials decided to delay the match.

Serena teamed with her sister Venus to win the 1999 French Open women's doubles title.

> I can't imagine playing with anybody else. Just the way it is. We do so well together. I know no matter what I do out there, Serena's always going to be behind me and there for me.
> —Venus Williams, www.venusserenafans.com, 1/26/01

The players waited 20 minutes for the rain to stop. Serena and Venus were eager to finish the match. But Hingis and Kournikova began playing better. The Williams sisters held a 6-5 lead. They were serving for the win. But Hingis and Kournikova tied the set at 6-6. They then won the tiebreaker when Serena hit a volley wide.

The match was close in the final set. Hingis and Kournikova took a 5-4 lead. They had a chance to serve for the win. But Serena and Venus won the next two games. They took a 7-6 lead. They then won all of the points in the final game. On the last point, Venus hit a strong backhand volley that Kournikova returned into the net. Serena and Venus had won. They were the French Open women's doubles champions.

About Serena and Venus Williams

The Williams sisters are two of the best and most exciting women's tennis players in the

The Williams sisters are two of the most successful athletes in the world.

world. They compete in singles, women's doubles, and mixed doubles. They each have won Grand Slam events in singles. Together, they have won all four Grand Slam events in doubles. In 2000, they won the Olympic gold medal in women's doubles.

Serena and Venus are two of the most powerful women ever to play tennis. Venus once hit a serve that traveled 127 miles (204 kilometers) per hour. No other woman has ever had a serve that powerful in a match. Serena also has a fast serve. Her serves almost always travel more than 100 miles (161 kilometers) per hour.

The Williams sisters also are successful off the court. Venus endorses Reebok shoes and equipment. She appears in TV commercials for Reebok. Reebok pays her millions of dollars to endorse and use their products. The deal is the largest endorsement contract in women's sports. Serena endorses equipment such as Puma shoes and Wilson athletic equipment. Together, the sisters endorse Avon products and Wrigley's Doublemint Gum.

CAREER STATISTICS

Venus and Serena

Women's Tennis Association Records

Venus			Serena		
Year	W-L	Rank	Year	W-L	Rank
1994	1-1	-	1994	-	-
1995	2-3	204	1995	-	-
1996	2-5	204	1996	-	-
1997	19-13	22	1997	3-2	99
1998	53-13	5	1998	26-11	20
1999	16-13	3	1999	41-7	4
2000	41-4	3	2000	37-8	6
2001*	46-5	4	2001*	35-7	7
Career*	180-57	4	Career*	142-35	7

*Through 9/18/01

CHAPTER 2

The Early Years

Venus was born June 17, 1980, in Lynwood, California. Serena was born September 26, 1981, in Saginaw, Michigan. Their parents are Richard and Oracene Williams. Richard managed a security business and Oracene was a nurse. Serena and Venus have three older sisters. Their names are Yetunde, Isha, and Lyndrea.

Growing up in Compton

Serena and Venus grew up in Compton, California. This city is near Los Angeles. Many people who live in Compton have little money. Tennis was not a popular sport there.

Richard Williams taught Venus and Serena to play tennis.

Richard sometimes watched tennis on TV. He knew that top tennis players made a great deal of money. He decided to teach his youngest daughters to play tennis.

Richard began to teach Venus to play tennis when she was 4. The courts in Compton were old and in poor shape. But Venus and Richard practiced often. A year later, Serena joined the practices.

When Venus was 8, she met men's tennis stars Pete Sampras and John McEnroe. Many tennis experts believe that Sampras and McEnroe are two of the best tennis players ever. Sampras and McEnroe were teaching young players about the game. They played tennis with Venus. After the practice, Venus told Richard that she thought she could have beaten McEnroe.

Venus continued to work on her skills. Tennis experts soon noticed her talent. *The New York Times* published two stories about Venus when she was 10.

Richard and Venus practiced playing tennis almost every day.

Venus got most of the attention when the sisters were young. But Serena also was developing into a good tennis player. The sisters began taking part in junior competitions. In 1991, Venus was ranked No. 1 in the southern California girls 12 years and under division. Serena was ranked No. 1 in the division for girls 10 and under.

Improving Skills

In 1991, the Williams family moved to Palm Beach Gardens, Florida. Venus and Serena stopped playing in junior tournaments. Richard wanted them to concentrate on professional careers. He did not believe playing in junior tournaments would help the girls become better.

The sisters started practicing harder than ever. Richard hired Richard Macci to coach the sisters. Macci and the girls practiced six hours each day, six days each week. But the girls did not play in any public tournaments during this time.

In 1992, Venus and Serena played against each other in an exhibition match in Hilton Head, South Carolina. Venus was 11 and Serena was 10. They played doubles with two famous tennis players. Venus teamed with Rosie Casals. Serena and Billie Jean King formed the other team. Serena and King won the match. But tennis experts were impressed with both girls.

Venus and Serena practiced against one another while they lived in Florida.

CHAPTER 3

Professional Tennis

Venus played in her first professional tournament on October 31, 1994, in Oakland, California. She was 14 years old. The event was her first public tournament in more than three years.

Venus beat Shaun Stafford in her first match. Her second-round opponent was Arantxa Sanchez Vicario. Sanchez Vicario was ranked No. 2 in the world. Venus played well early in the match. She led 6-3, 3-0. But Sanchez Vicario won 12 straight games to win the match.

Venus played in her first professional match on October 31, 1994.

Tennis fans quickly noticed Venus' talent. She played much better than most players her age. Many people also thought that she was one of the most powerful female players they had seen. Venus signed an endorsement contract with Reebok a few months later. The five-year contract was worth $12 million.

Venus did not join the Women's Tennis Association (WTA) tour full time. Richard did not think that she was ready. She and Serena played in several professional tournaments during the next few years. But neither sister won any of these events.

On the Tour

Venus joined the WTA tour full time in 1997. She had little success early in the year. Venus entered the U.S. Open in August. This tournament is one of four Grand Slam events. The other Grand Slam events are the Australian Open, Wimbledon, and the French Open.

Venus entered the U.S. Open ranked No. 66 in the world. She had not advanced to a

Venus advanced to the championship match of the 1997 U.S. Open.

tournament final all year. Few people expected her to do well in the Open.

Venus was excited to be playing in the U.S. Open. She played some of her best tennis ever. She won her first five matches. In the semifinals, she beat Irina Spirlea 7-6, 4-6, 7-6. The win put her in the championship match. Venus became the first black woman to play in the final in 40 years.

Venus faced Martina Hingis in the U.S. Open final. Hingis was the No. 1 player in the world. Hingis won the first set 6-0. Venus played better in the second set. But Hingis still won 6-4 to earn the U.S. Open title.

Serena's Turn

Serena also joined the women's tour in 1997. Her first event was on October 27 in Moscow, Russia. She lost her first match to Kimberly Po 3-6, 6-7.

Serena's next event was the Ameritech Cup in Chicago, Illinois. She entered the tournament ranked No. 304 in the world. She beat Elena Likhovtseva in the first round. She then played seventh-ranked Mary Pierce. Serena surprised tennis fans by winning the match 6-3, 7-6.

Serena's next match was against Monica Seles. Seles was the No. 4 player in the world. Seles won the first set 6-4. But Serena won the next two sets 6-1, 6-1 to advance to the tournament final. Serena became the lowest

Serena easily won her first match at the 1998 Australian Open.

ranked player ever to beat two top-10 players in the same tournament. But Serena did not win the tournament. Lindsey Davenport won the final 6-4, 6-4.

Growing Fame
Until January 1998, Venus and Serena had never played each other in a professional event. That fact changed at the Australian Open.

Venus and Serena both won their first-round matches. They were paired against each other for the second round. Venus won the match easily. But she then lost to Davenport in the quarterfinals.

Later that month, Serena signed an endorsement deal with Puma. Puma agreed to pay Serena $12 million if she made the WTA's top 10.

Venus won her first professional tournament in February. The tournament was the IGA Tennis Classic in Oklahoma City, Oklahoma. Venus and Serena also won their first doubles title at the event. They became the first sisters to win a professional doubles title.

Venus and Serena each played mixed doubles in 1998. Venus teamed with Justin Gimelstob. Together, they won the mixed doubles titles at the Australian Open and the French Open. Serena's partner was Max Mirnyi. Serena and Mirnyi won the mixed doubles titles at the U.S. Open and Wimbledon.

Venus beat Serena in the second round of the 1998 Australian Open.

Making History

On February 28, 1999, Venus won the IGA Tennis Classic in Oklahoma City. On the same day, Serena won the Gaz de France Open in Paris. It was Serena's first professional title. The two also became the first sisters to win professional tournaments on the same day.

On March 28, 1999, Venus and Serena again played each other. They had both reached the final of the Lipton Championships in Key Biscayne, Florida. Venus won the first set 6-1. Serena won the second set 6-4. The third set was close. But Venus scored eight of the final nine points to win 6-4.

Serena did not win the title. But she was happy for her sister. She also knew that her skills were improving. She was ready to begin a great summer of tennis.

Venus held the trophy at the Lipton Championships after defeating Serena in the final.

CHAPTER 4

Grand Slams

Serena and Venus teamed to win the French Open doubles title in June 1999. Their tennis skills continued to improve. They were quickly becoming two of the most famous tennis players in the world.

Serena Wins the U.S. Open

In September, the sisters entered the U.S. Open. Both of them advanced to the semifinals. Serena won her semifinal match against Davenport. But Venus lost her match to Hingis. Serena faced Hingis in the championship match.

Serena beat Martina Hingis in the final of the 1999 U.S. Open.

Venus and Serena won the 1999 U.S. Open women's doubles title.

Hingis was the No. 1 player in the world. But Serena was confident. She won the first set 6-3. She then won a close second set 7-6 to win the title. It was the first singles Grand Slam title either sister had won. Serena also became the second black woman to win a Grand Slam singles title. Althea Gibson won five titles in the 1950s. Serena and Venus also won the U.S. Open doubles title.

Venus felt bad after the loss. She said that she expected to win a Grand Slam before her sister. Venus took some time away from tennis later that year. Many people believed that Venus would retire. Richard Williams even said that he hoped Venus would stop playing.

Venus was not ready to retire. She returned to the tour in 2000. But she did not play well in her first few matches. Some tennis experts believed that she would never be as good as she had once been.

Return of Venus

Few people expected Venus to do well at Wimbledon in July 2000. But Venus knew that she still had the ability to be a great player.

Venus played the best tennis of her career at Wimbledon. She advanced to the semifinals. There, she faced Serena. Venus defeated her sister and advanced to the final.

Venus faced defending Wimbledon champion Davenport in the final. Venus won the first set 6-3. Davenport took a 3-1 lead in the second set. But Venus came back to force a tiebreaker. She easily won the tiebreaker. Venus jumped into the air after Davenport hit the final shot into the net. She finally had won a Grand Slam title.

Venus continued to play well after her Wimbledon victory. At one point, she won 32 straight matches and three straight titles. She then entered the U.S. Open. Again, she reached the final against Davenport. She won 6-4, 7-5 to claim her second Grand Slam title.

The Olympics

In July 2000, Venus and Serena were selected to represent the United States in the 2000 Olympic Games. The games took place in Australia during the end of September.

Venus continued her winning streak at the Olympics. She won the Olympic gold medal in women's singles by beating Russia's Elena Dementieva 6-2, 6-4.

Venus held the Venus Rosewater Dish after defeating Lindsey Davenport in the 2000 Wimbledon final.

This is the one moment in time for me, for my country, for my family, for the team.... I watched the Olympics at home when I was a kid, and it was one of my dreams for my dad to win an Olympic medal. It means a lot.
—Venus Williams, MSNBC.com, 9/28/00

One day later, Venus and Serena played in the women's doubles gold medal match. They faced the Dutch team of Kristie Boogert and Miriam Oremans. The Williams sisters easily won the match 6-1, 6-1. On the last point, Venus hit a serve that traveled 115 miles (185 kilometers) per hour. Boogert barely returned the serve. Serena then smashed an overhead slam to end the match. The sisters carried the U.S. flag on their shoulders to celebrate.

Venus had become the first woman to win the gold medal in singles and doubles since Helen Wills in 1924. After the Olympics, Venus was ranked No. 3 in the world. This ranking was the highest of her career. In December 2000, *Sports Illustrated* magazine named her Sportswoman of the Year.

Venus and Serena held the American flag after they won the Olympic gold medal for women's doubles.

CHAPTER 5

Serena and Venus Today

The Williams sisters remain two of the world's best female tennis players. They are two of the most popular female athletes in the world.

Success in 2001

Serena and Venus continued their success in 2001. Each sister won a tournament early in the year. Venus beat Jennifer Capriati to win the Ericsson Open. Venus lost the first set 4-6. But she came back to win the next two 6-1, 7-6. Serena won the Masters Series

Venus and Serena remain two of the best players in women's tennis.

tournament in March. In the final, Serena lost the first set to Kim Clijsters 4-6. She won the last two sets 6-4, 6-2 for the title.

The Williams sisters also have faced problems in 2001. Many tennis fans have booed them on the court. These fans disagree with things that Richard has said about his daughters and their opponents. Other fans say that the sisters act too confident off the court. Serena was booed loudly in her win over Clijsters in the Masters Series final.

Venus returned to Wimbledon to defend her title in 2001. She did not play well in the early rounds. But she still was able to win her matches. Serena also advanced through the early rounds. But she was ill during her quarterfinal match against Capriati. Capriati won the match 6-7, 7-5, 6-3. Venus beat Davenport in the semifinals 6-2, 6-7, 6-1 to advance to the final.

Venus faced Justine Henin in the final. Venus won the first set 6-1. But Henin played better in the second set and won 6-3. Venus

Serena beat Kim Clijsters to win the 2001 Masters Series title.

played well in the final set to win 6-0. Once again, she was the Wimbledon champion.

Venus and Serena played well in the 2001 U.S. Open. They both advanced to the final. On September 8, they faced each other for the U.S. Open title.

Venus easily won the first set 6-2. The second set was closer. The sisters were tied 4-4. But Venus then won the last two games to claim another Grand Slam title. Venus hugged Serena at center court after the match.

Off the Court

Serena and Venus have earned millions of dollars playing tennis. They have earned millions more in endorsement deals. Richard and Oracene still manage and coach their daughters. At least one parent tries to attend every tournament the girls take part in.

The sisters do not spend all of their time on a tennis court. They listen to pop music and go to movies together. Venus enjoys reading and

Venus won her second straight Wimbledon title in 2001.

collecting old furniture. Serena spends time with her dogs. She also plays the guitar.

Many people still think that Venus will retire soon. In July 2001, Richard again said that he thinks Venus may be near the end of her career. Venus is interested in fashion. She designs many of the tennis outfits that she wears during matches. She hopes to start a career in fashion after she is finished playing tennis.

Serena plans to play tennis for years to come. She also is interested in art. She takes art classes at the Art Institute of Florida.

Serena and Venus know that they have opportunities that most other people do not have. They remember growing up in a poor neighborhood. They often give time and money to charities. They often play for free in charity matches. The money from ticket sales goes to help people in need. Serena and Venus know that they can use their fame to improve other people's lives.

Venus and Serena enjoy spending time together off the tennis court.

Career Highlights

1980—Venus is born June 17 in Lynwood, California.

1981—Serena is born September 26 in Saginaw, Michigan.

1988—Venus practices with men's stars John McEnroe and Pete Sampras.

1992—Serena and Venus play against each other in an exhibition doubles match; Serena's team wins.

1994—Venus wins her first professional match in Oakland, California.

1997—Venus loses to Martina Hingis in the U.S. Open final; Serena joins the WTA tour; Serena beats two top-10 players in her second professional event.

1998—Venus wins her first pro singles title at the IGA Tennis Classic; she pairs with Serena to win the doubles title in the same tournament.

1999—Venus and Serena win the French Open women's doubles title; Serena beats Hingis to win the U.S. Open.

2000—Venus beats Lindsay Davenport in the finals of Wimbledon and the U.S. Open; Serena and Venus win the Olympic gold medal in women's doubles; Venus wins the Olympic gold medal in women's singles.

2001—Venus defends her Wimbledon title by beating Justine Henin; Venus beats Serena in the U.S. Open final.

Words to Know

contract (KON-trakt)—a legal agreement between two groups or individuals

endorse (en-DORSS)—to sponsor a product by appearing in advertisements

exhibition match (ek-suh-BISH-uhn MACH)—a match played only for show; exhibition matches do not count toward player rankings.

professional (pruh-FESH-uh-nuhl)—an athlete who is paid to participate in a sport

quarterfinal (KWOR-tur-fye-nuhl)—a match to determine which player advances to the semifinal round; eight players compete in the quarterfinal round.

semifinal (SEM-ee-fye-nuhl)—a match to determine which player advances to the championship match; four players compete in the semifinal round.

To Learn More

Aronson, Virginia. *Venus & Serena Williams.* Women Who Win. Philadelphia: Chelsea House Publishers, 2001.

Asirvatham, Sandy. *Venus Williams.* Black Americans of Achievement. Philadelphia: Chelsea House Publishers, 2001.

Morgan, Terri. *Venus and Serena Williams: Grand Slam Sisters.* Minneapolis: Lerner Publications, 2001.

Stewart, Mark. *Venus & Serena Williams: Sisters in Arms.* Tennis's New Wave. Brookfield, Conn.: Millbrook Press, 2000.

Useful Addresses

ATP Tennis International Headquarters
201 ATP Tour Boulevard
Ponte Vedra Beach, FL 32082

Women's Tennis Association
1266 East Main Street
4th Floor
Stamford, CT 06902-3546

Internet Sites

CNN/Sports Illustrated—Tennis
http://sportsillustrated.cnn.com/tennis

ESPN.com—Serena Williams
http://espn.go.com/tennis/s/wta/profiles/
swilliams.html

ESPN.com—Venus Williams
http://espn.go.com/tennis/s/wta/profiles/
vwilliams.html

VenusSerenaFans.com
http://www.venusserenafans.com

Index

Ameritech Cup, 20
Australian Open, 18,
    21–22

Capriati, Jennifer, 35, 36
Casals, Rosie, 14

Davenport, Lindsey, 21,
    22, 27, 29–30, 36

endorsements, 8, 18, 22,
    38
Ericsson Open, 35

French Open, 5–6, 18,
    22, 27

Gaz de France Open, 25
Gibson, Althea, 28

Henin, Justine, 36
Hingis, Martina, 5–6, 20,
    27–28
hobbies, 38, 41

IGA Tennis Classic, 22, 25

King, Billie Jean, 14
Kournikova, Anna, 5–6

Lipton Championships, 25

Macci, Richard, 14
Masters Series, 35–36
McEnroe, John, 12

Olympic Games, 8, 30, 32

Sampras, Pete, 12
Seles, Monica, 20

U.S. Open, 18–19, 20, 22,
    27–28, 30, 38

Williams, Oracene, 11, 38
Williams, Richard, 11, 12,
    14, 18, 29, 36, 38, 41
Wimbledon, 18, 22,
    29–30, 36, 38